On the Count of None

for m.

Contents

Prologue

A song is played.

A violin is heard.

On the forestage, a dollhouse—
an orange glow in the windows,
the air of a dream.

From the right Ellen, the maidservant, enters.

The curtains are drawn.

The violin plays on.

Heist

This day is a string of jewellery-store robberies
and we stand motionless.

A suffocating pause,
a crescendo on our breaths.

We gave ourselves over.
We fully submitted.

The stillness that overtook us
was borrowed from a book.

Epoch

Teens of the new millennium
tattoo their inner thighs
and mouth the words
to shoddy pleas—
scandalized confessions lifted
a thousand feet above.

Worldly or Otherwise

On this side of the world we put things in order:
hairpins, asthma inhalers, glasses of milk.
We edit our obituaries and euthanize our old ambitions.
We underwrite our uncertainties and pause to remember a voice.
On this side of the world we believe in suicide the old-fashioned way.

On this side of the world we strike out inscriptions left in books.
We keep your rumours at the edge of our vision.
We cast out broken skeletons and infiltrate audible gasps.
It's another type of sinking—here, on this side of the world.

Heart Sound

A half portrait of Ellen,
all out-at-the-elbows.

On the morning of her conception,
a call from the kitchen.

Her sister strikes a match,
fills her cup,
splits her dosage.

She is the kitchen door pulled shut,
the kitchen window pried open.

A bell rings in the hall.
The window is opened.
A lit lamp,
an outdoor dress,
and a well-bound book
rest on the kitchen table.

After a short silence,
a key is turned, a door is locked.
Ellen enters from the left,
brings her hands to her face
and draws a heavy breath.

Aries (March 21–April 19)

If you are not yet moving at top speed, you very soon will be.

Reach out to a close ally.

Consult an expert at low volume.

The results will be pleasing: an abundance of greenery in the shadows of Venus.

Be prepared for a strong reaction.

Full Disclosure

On the subject of her own gifts
she will often look you
dead in the eye
and tell you
she's blown her own mind.

Origins

Very briefly:

any number of enthusiasts
and several eminent men of the universities
never quite abandon
those early calls of credence.

Birdsong
and the glint of an insect's wing
on the voyage of the *Beagle*
are the best and safest clues.

A faster hound!
A woollier sheep!
A friendly cat!
A fire-bellied newt!

Animated beings
sharpening their claws
on finer points,
throwing light into the shadows.

In smaller quarters
a divine spark
is the descendent of
an earlier one.

Hibernation

Our winter wardrobes awoke from hibernation,
emptied their pockets of last year's receipts,
and crawled into our closets.

My Unravelling

Well, maybe I did
clamour around the subtle sense of luxury.

During the angular movement
I disfigured a sandscript [sic] scholar.

. But maybe I didn't
abandon the child prodigy
and the metabolic processes
like two drops of sadness
abundant on the teaspoon.

[Pee break.]

Our mutual decay
and your untying of my apron strings
occur each Wednesday
or when hanging from the branches.

Taurus (April 20–May 20)

You will be wise to make yourself available to a new friend this month.

Expand your relationships beyond the limitations of sentients.

Consider:

squeaky door hinges,

ornate cake stands,

abandoned electronics.

The Dollhouse

A maid-servant (Ellen)—her husband must never know
how an empty cigar box and a broken hairpin
were recovered on the ledge of the front window.
Near the window a rocking chair, and along the wall
a round table—a black cross marks the door
that leads to Helmer's study.
The approved remedy for loneliness is
a stiffening expression, a bedfast songbird.
Somewhat by surprise, a lark, toneless as a tarantella,
enters the dollhouse in Act II
to grasp the hairpin, unsettle the cigar box.
In the next masquerade, Ellen will be all but invisible
and Helmer's three children will cross the stage,
extend their doll-like hands, and receive, without realizing it,
a certainty of thought.

The Delicate Thing

I keep thinking

How it felt

To stand beside you

On that quiet morning

With the coffee brewing

And the water boiling

And the eggs tapping

And you avoiding

My outstretched hand

With your stretched-out truth.

It gets ground up.

In your kitchen

With each drawer open

And the throats clearing

And the eyes lowering

And the nostrils flaring

And the cheeks flushing

And the doors slamming

And the darkness deepening

And the dust stirring

And the clouds bursting

And the thunder roaring.

It's nice to stand beside you.

The Nature of the Culture

Once marooned, the humans enter the landscape.

Starting a culture is an epiphany.

A hard-earned dollar will buy you a stereo headset,
a temporary tattoo, a shoeshine, and instant coffee.

Service for the solitary is an around-the-clock operation.

A necessary business for the mothers who speed away
to feed their daughters.

For the soft underbellies of well-dressed husbands.

For the authoritarian personalities who forge their identities.

For the dignified treatment of profitable celebrities.

Obituary for Zeus

1.

Here lies Zeus, a true believer
who wears this trinket as a talisman.
A visionary who became
office-wide famous
for jumping through the horns
of a bull.

2.

Thunderbolt levelled in his raised right hand
and decorated with the flowers of another era.
Disguised as a snow-white bull
among the milk-white cattle.

3.

Never thinking of his soul
and unconnected with the souls of the dead.
A god from whose body corn grows.
The youngest of his siblings.
An isolated fantasy in his real life
who is condemned to walk,
forlorn, down the high road.

Our Things in Boxes

in
odd
corners

an error in the record

in
odd
corners

a continuous applause

in
odd
corners

a wooden sailing ship

in
odd
corners

a sleight of hand
a passing grade

in
odd
corners

a dropped potato
the heat of the hat

in
odd
corners

a nail on the head
a wagon at bay

in
odd
corners

two birds
one flock

in
odd
corners

one arm
three legs

in
odd
corners

more sliced bread
than you can swallow

in
odd
corners

my day job

in
odd
corners

a rocker
a boat
a single piece of cake

Bleat

Beep! Beep!

Hungry women, imaginary thunderstorms.

Beep! Beep!

A ghostly enchilada, a powerful skillet.

Beep! Beep!

Fragrant shower caps and a hole in the wall.

Beep!

Moon roof.

Beep!

Satellite dish.

Beep. Beep.

Postman's autograph!

Gemini (May 21–June 20)

This month you will rely

on a sturdy internal frame.

Use your fortitude to protect

your internal organs

from the pull of gravity.

As much as possible be on the lookout for

sheep herders or

free radicals.

All signs suggest

a resurgence in uncertainty.

Sanatorium

He is known for grey granite pedestals,
acid reflux
& a phobia of inky fingertips.

He is known for fanciful Victorian gazebos,
a defibrillated heartbeat, a high-fibre diet
& a barely legible script.

He is known for poorly tuned vocal cords,
the alienated Iroquois
& an ataxic gait.

He is known for coming-of-age literature,
a long-handled shoehorn
& a Plains of Abraham birthmark.

But mostly he is known for his 18th-century stamp collection,
a white hospital gown, unusual swelling
& a shortness of breath.

Urban Everything

On deserted beaches the living carry out a tiny community,
sing for hundreds, then come back to urban everything.

Sinuous dresses knotted from lace
cling tightly to a tiny bodice.

Among all the sheer
black-and-white pantsuits with punk-referenced kilts:
true to the heritage.

In watching all this,
now in the realms of fantasy,
risen from the deep,

a sea-goddess or shipwreck
the finale in the crashing, foaming surf.

> *Add these dates to your agenda:*
> > *September 14th — move-in day*
> > *October 27th — housewarming party*
> > *November 13th — book launch*
> > *December 23rd — tiny bodice adjustments*
> > *January 17th — shipwreck expedition*
> > *February 2nd — fantasy exploration*
> > *March 23rd — sea goddess beauty pageant*
> > *April 7th — finale in the crashing, foaming surf*

The Scissor Grinder's Guild

On the day the regiment least resembled an army,
tearful women waved from the shore.
Officers, young and properly inexperienced,
removed their neckties.
Scissor grinders bartered their prognosis for collateral ligaments.
Minute muscle contractions infiltrated enemy ranks
and twitched in trepidation.
Stretcher-bearers,
their eyes a visionary blue,
threw down their rib cages.

99 cents

fresh

little

necks

The Dollhouse

Within the variability of everything, our righthand lady (Ellen)
readjusts the value of the thing.
Does she have a full scope of the situation?
Has she accounted for all the details?
In her mind, a day is seven hours
and she figures it will take five days.
Here in this house she has learned a good lesson
and one day a statue may be carved in her likeness.
A surgeon, a neurologist, a historian, and a dancer—
she is almost always any of these things.
In staff meetings and washroom stalls,
Ellen forms a persuasive stance.
Decisive moves at precise locations
have helped to soften the sharpest edges.

In Act III, Ellen will suppress a smile, strike a match,
and submit her final notice before slipping into the shadows.

Cancer (June 21–July 22)

Today your accomplishments will be celebrated

with leather-gloved applause.

Say yes to the proposals of half-siblings

or bachelors with a strong constitution.

Stay away from stonyfish and fruitbones.

Listening for the Extraterrestrial Message

Citizens of the Cosmos:

The absent are always wrong in dealing from the bottom of the deck. Under our hats—a calm intensity. A eureka moment, a revelation in the scriptures, flickers in and out, like brainwaves and heartbeats; strange goings-on between the orbits. Intercepted transmissions:

greetings in 24 human languages, strands of esoteric lore, the strength of one man's fist! When listening for the extraterrestrial message, the most ancient rules apply.

Measured in hours and degrees, sermons on the stones are passed by without further assessment,

while the brightest stars in each hemisphere are plotted on the charts. With proper orientation, the stars of last season become signposts and pointers. Use this map to orient your location:

15 degrees from the horizon
or three steps forward and
one shaky inhalation.

These are the coordinates where we rise and set. Our horizon shifted, our axis tilted.

Leo (July 23–August 22)

You will notice a difference in how people approach you this month.

Those with ill intentions may be drawn to your charisma.

Cling tightly to your old-fashioned mahogany values.

Train yourself in the prevention of a paradox.

You have a handshake that makes sinners squirm.

Credo

for Stuart

Abundant in your hand—
a lightness of being
an amazing shard of grace
the bleating of goats
your coming of age
your middle-aged nephew
a concession to outrage
your missionary zeal
the origins of life
a plausible suggestion
the cultivation of coherence.

The cheese stands alone.

Integers and Dendrites

Your stoned brain was right
until the next feeding
we all sat in anticipation
like a third-order neuron
before synapsing in the thalamus.

When you wake
you eat.

Full of words and motor impulses
integers and dendrites
whose innervation stops
short of stimulation.

money in the meter

for Michael

In accordance with your core principles, my job has been to keep you alive. Hardly permissible under law but from the business side of things, this affiliation has been lucrative for both of us. When I cannot find you, I know where to look: between our resting oars, beneath our neighbour's prying eyes, within the curtain's creases, next to the fallen markers, along the street with these warm bodies. Inside each of these dimensions, you deliver on your calling.

Overheard by others: our steady breaths, our pumping blood, electrical impulses and chemical reactions.

Virgo (August 23–September 22)

Do not get discouraged by a setback this month.

Instead, confer with

a boardwalk vendor

or a simple mechanical lever system.

You may be given

an extra measure of

the milk of human kindness.

Thievery

A dream atmosphere is achieved at the apex,

stolen from a secured cargo area,
disarmed by a police officer.

Bitter masterminds who,
guarded from birth,

abscond with curiosities and wonders

worth rupees and jewels,
sapphires and diamonds,

or, at least,

one Canadian dollar.

Sandscript

Millions of believers—
and four imaginary pairs of shoes
slip past doorways
stirring dust beneath their feet.

Libra (September 24–October 23)

Today your name will resonate

through thin-walled chambers and

post-war taverns.

Don't postpone a true believer.

Don't betray a complicated matter.

Understand that every other name

begins and ends

with dirt in the sky.

Made in the USA

Our founding fathers
the fugitives of the spacious west
the busters of the first frontier
the survivors of a lengthy labour
the brokers of a darker era.

Our founding fathers
reschedule the seasons
unholster their torpedoes
compass their confidence
and absorb some other form.

The boggy wetness underfoot is the compass to the season. Tiny variations too smooth and too sure are like a charging atom or a youthful second cousin whose confidence is cast to shore.

Western shadows creep across the valley. The eastern rain holds up. The frontier, like a heavy brow, labours and awakens the sky, the sky, the sky, more blue and still than ever before.

Uppercrest

When the cooler climates came, I gave up all modern conveniences. In moonlit nights and along Georgian Bay, I traded in my well-groomed thoughts for wild abandon, bare instincts, a sporting interest. Tucked away in canyons and around the archipelago, I earned a decent grade mapping flights, skinning hides, charting stars.

I kept a clean camp.

I improvised a fishing hook.

The upper crests of the escarpment scraped the sky, cliffs framed the shores, and I removed my shoes and socks to be born again in the grotto.

Your New Home

for Christine

You, invaded.

As wise as rust,
as red as Confucius.

Lessons in articulation.
Outfits,
designer infants.

Better Than Okay

I found myself in pursuit of the sky, clad in brilliance, a
spectrum of colours—unabused, unabashed.

It became graphic. Several young people have dispelled the truth
behind the atrocities and further research revealed a
conclusion for which we simply do not have the tools.

In a dream, an owl. Black and white surround her kaleidoscope
eyes. As we attempt to photograph her, she changes from beast
to human, a life-sized Cuban, a bambi-eyed charmer.

In the months since we met last winter, she has taken to off-the-
books cab driving and often gazes heavenward in exasperation.
No more to attend the tap-on-the-shoulder parties with loyal
optimists among the complainers.

The money she sends home will buy her son new shoes and
afford her a glimpse of the turquoise sea.

Scorpio (October 23–November 21)

Avoid confrontation with someone with whom you share
controversial ideas.

Instead try to appeal

to a small person in a quiet river

or a clan of Viking descendants.

The key to your happiness is in

the mouth of the zoologist,

a plumber's tool belt, or

old reliable standbys.

Witness comic activity

in the most sensitive area of your chart.

The Dollhouse

Ellen, all at sea, begs us to tell her what we want.
A home in the country? A modest house in the city?
The questions drum in head and heart, and Ellen,
sitting at the piano, plays a chord to clear the air.
Until long after midnight, and well before the ending note,
Ellen, buried in thought, is mapping flights and mooring boats.

Between the sofa and the side door, and nearer
to the front window: a bookcase.
Ellen classifies her showily bound books.
Ellen adds our names to her do-to list.
Secretly and truthfully, Ellen draws a heavy breath.
Alone in the room, and before the curtains draw,
Ellen slows the tempo, extends the solo, and hums the final note.

Yours

for Nelson

I

tried

out

your

big

sigh.

Sagittarius (November 22–December 21)

You will find it necessary to restructure part of your day-to-day routine.

Defer to a household deity

or a small portion of humankind.

A new beginning becomes possible

when you take a quick break from the worst of the species.

This week: rediscover the relic of your youth

or some other thing

chopped up in the kitchen.

The Thing About Me

This may be of interest to no one:

tiny variations
and my stray grey hairs
stoop an olive shoulder.

larger and stronger
my sudden leaps
grasp at revelation.

my clenched fists
and your flattened breaths
are our black Cadillacs.

it's been one week.
I still suspect
we liveth and believeth.

shifts in style
and an old suede shoe?
I nod yes.

seven days after
my eureka moment
a period of maximum confusion.

it takes bodies
or one final trust
to soften the blow.

where the crowds are,
one drawn-out note
is born again.

sternly and profoundly
I advise
a minor deviation.

my first encounter
bespeaks deceit
and higher honour.

a short snooze
and your obscure origins
follow us and bother us.

additional considerations:
—a love poem for Michael
—a moored emotion.

a book I never read
and these tiny objects
trophy my to-do list.

secretly and truthfully
your esteem
is better than okay.

hands down
fresh shouts
follow me around.

a few blocks over
a sparkling version of myself
sits with a quiet intensity.

Steady and Direct

Our well-groomed thoughts
born again and
restored to human form

a general drift
at a dollar rate

overbought and oversold

savage enough

and close

but not too close.

Capricorn (December 22–January 19)

This month you may feel overlooked

by an influential person.

You will be mistaken for someone

whose back-of-the-head

looks remarkably like your own.

Who Besides Me?

You at the helm—

windblown and wayward,

a dark sky observer.

Below these decks

address these hands—

disorderly and ungloved.

Heavy-handed but

adrift, afoot, abreast,

a sacker of cities.

Capsized or baptized

I take the fall.

Putting Your House in Order

for Kristen

Stow away
your caribou-skin boots
a houndstooth jacket
some segments of people
my upper hand.

Add to the ledger
subtle style shifts
neonates and not-so-newborns
a wide variety of topics
a bikini emoji
and certainty on a cellular level.

Aquarius (January 20–February 18)

You radiate a willingness to undermine.

Support a close friend who may try to extract the miners' discovery.

Demonstrate your esteem

with a chorus of obscurity

or crumbs for birds.

He or she likes what he or she sees.

Siege

after James Tate

I am not a weapons expert. And yet, every evening I study *The Art of War*. (Once I translated the entire text from Chinese to English to Chinese again.) And every morning I closely regard the military and diplomatic engagements between squirrels in my neighbourhood. (The browntails appear to be a mammal with a genuine authority over military matters.) In the afternoons I flip through rifle catalogues. They enhance my lust for life yet lower my blood pressure. When my daughter, the general, interrupts my studies, she always salutes me before retreating to the kitchen.

Woman Does Backflip Before Slipping into Shadows

Dear Abby,
How do I measure
Some level of risk
A comfortable silence
And a single sailing season?

How, Abby,
Do I wrestle
This pirate stronghold
An instant foreboding
And a legendary creature?

Dear, dear Abby
Is there a fine line
Between a daylong battle
And a misty morning?

Abby—
Sun filters through leaves
Snow covers all in sight
I hear popping and crackling
As Mom drops bacon into the pan.

Life is an expenditure
And I need some capital.

Sincerely,
Ellen

Extract

unauthorized drilling
off the shores of our kitchen
has devastated the natural habitat
of teaspoons and
spatulas.

The Precise Order of Things

after Lisa Jarnot

On this most perfect hill with these most perfect dogs, I found the perfect parliament. In these most perfect pockets, I found the perfect sentiment. Within an almost perfect stethoscope, I heard a perfect chorus. Next to a perfect stream, a flawless source. Through hoops of perfect fire, I earned a decent grade. How terrific it is to find an already perfect blueprint. A perfect whistle. A perfect watchmaker. A perfect watch. Across a perfect street, an orange cat licks a wounded paw. The street light flickers on and off. A crumpled page of yesterday's newspaper is swept across your feet. You bend down to pick it up. A perfect editorial! (Between you and me—a perfect publication.) Next to a perfect stream, a table. Upon a steady table, a pawn. Anoint the king, attack the bishop. Blindfold the perfect child. Shoplift the perfect present. Exchange the perfect _____. A perfect queen, a perfect knight, a perfect rook. A pawn. Perfect the perfect adjective to write the perfect poem.

Pisces (February 19–March 20)

The focus today is on

the expansion of your oesophagus.

Ask yourself how

millions of sensory receptors

detect change.

Monitor such things as

temperature, light, and sound.

Outsource your nerve impulses.

Safeguard the complexities of your internal
environment.

Rendered

Translated into twenty-four different languages:
—a steady stare
—a few new faces
—a faithful few
—a long reflection
—fits of rage
—snails (small and see-through)
—a specimen collection
—generalists and specialists
—aggrievements and disaggrievements
—exceeding expectations
—a history going back one hundred years
—adverse incidents
—a slip-resistant shoe
—a critical eye
—a prompt response
—a port of entry
—a best-case scenario
—shoes in good repair
—the business side of things
—criminal activity
—my vital signs

Words to live by.

Memento

His collection of bird specimens
can be seen on the first floor of the house.
When the people left,
the breathing stopped.
A pair of sturdy shoes
moved farther up the St. Lawrence,
canonized with
other artifacts.

Epilogue

On the forestage—
Ellen in the dimness,
quietly dressed.

A match is struck,
a lamp is lit.

The kitchen table brightens.

Offstage
and under one's breath

a sigh,
escaped.

Notes & Acknowledgments

"The Precise Order of Things" was written after Lisa Jarnot's "Poem Beginning with a Line by Frank Lima" and borrows the first line of her "This Most Perfect Hill."

Henrik Ibsen's play *A Doll's House* inspired several poems here.

Many of these poems appeared first in the chapbook *On the Count of One* (Proper Tales Press) and *The Northern Testicle Review*. "The Dollhouse" (page 20) and "99 cents" were published by Puddles of Sky Press. A version of "The Thing About Me" appeared in *Train: a journal of investigation*. "My Unravelling" appeared on *The Week Shall Inherit The Verse* online.

Thank you, Christine Miscione and Nicholas Papaxanthos, for planting the seed.

Thank you, m society (whose identity I will never reveal), for your encouragement and inspiration.

Thank you to my family, for your steadfast support and cultivation of the uncanny.

My deepest gratitude to Feed Dog editor Stuart Ross, for his keen insight and perception, his commitment to my writing, and for stewarding me into the community of poetry and small press publishing.

Thank you, Michael, for your well-groomed thoughts and dapper edits, for teaching me to read and write poetry, and for your uncompromising support and faith in my work.

Allison Chisholm was born in Cobourg and lives in Kingston, Ontario. She played glockenspiel in the Hawaiian-Dream-Pop band SCUB. Her poetry has appeared in *The Northern Testicle Review*, *The Dollhouse* (Puddles of Sky Press) and *Train: a journal of investigation*. Her chapbook, *On the Count of One*, was published in 2017 (Proper Tales Press). She is the curator of the Museum of Tiny Objects.

Other Feed Dog Books from Anvil Press

"A Feed Dog Book" is an imprint of Anvil Press edited by Stuart Ross and dedicated to contemporary poetry under the influence of surrealism. We are particularly interested in seeing such manuscripts from members of diverse and marginalized communities. Write Stuart at razovsky@gmail.com.

The Least You Can Do Is Be Magnificent:
New & Selected Writings of Steve Venright
by Steve Venright,
compiled and with an afterword by Alessandro Porco
(2017)

I Heard Something
by Jaime Forsythe
(2018)

an imprint of Anvil Press